WATER FOR LIFE

BY VALERIE BODDEN

CREATIVE ● EDUCATION

Published by Creative Education
P.O. Box 227, Mankato, Minnesota 56002
Creative Education is an imprint of
The Creative Company
www.thecreativecompany.us

Design and production by The Design Lab
Art direction by Rita Marshall
Printed by Corporate Graphics in the
United States of America

Photographs by Alamy (Tor Eigeland, Eye
Ubiquitous, Images of Africa Photobank,
NASA), Corbis (Diego Azubel/epa, Bettmann,
Michael Christopher Brown, Philippe
Lissac/Godong, Michael T. Sedam), iStock-
photo (Andres Balcazar, Rob Broek, Robert
Churchill, Krzysztof Gawor, Michal Giedrojc,
Bill Grove, José Luis Gutiérrez, Chris Hepburn,
Matt Knannlein, Shannon Long, Johnny Lye,
Andreas Prott, Jorge Salcedo, Paolo Santoné,
Dean Turner, Frank Van Den Bergh)

Library of Congress
Cataloging-in-Publication Data
Bodden, Valerie.
Water for life / by Valerie Bodden.
p. cm. — (Earth issues)
Includes bibliographical references and index.
Summary: An examination of the shrinking
supplies of freshwater resources, exploring
how water has been polluted, diverted, and
over-consumed, as well as how better water
management contributes to a healthier planet.
ISBN 978-1-58341-986-1
1. Water resources development—Juvenile
literature. 2. Water supply—Juvenile literature.
3. Water consumption—Juvenile literature. I.
Title. II. Series.

HD1691.B62 2010
333.91—dc22   2009028054

CPSIA: 120109 PO1091
First Edition
9 8 7 6 5 4 3 2 1

Table of Contents

CHAPTER ONE

A Life-Sustaining Cycle......6

CHAPTER TWO

Using and Abusing Water.....14

CHAPTER THREE

A Dire Situation...........24

CHAPTER FOUR

Renewing the Resource......34

Glossary.......................45
Bibliography...................46
For Further Information........47
Index..........................48

Everything human beings need to survive—air to breathe, food to eat, water to drink—is found on Earth, and on Earth alone. Yet the very planet that sustains human life has come under threat because of human activities. Rivers are drying up as people divert water for their own use. Temperatures are warming as greenhouse gases such as carbon dioxide trap heat in the **atmosphere**. Species of plants and animals are disappearing as people destroy essential habitats. And the rate of many such changes appears to be accelerating. "If I had to use one word to describe the environmental state of the planet right now, I think I would say precarious," said population expert Robert Engelman. "It isn't doomed. It isn't certainly headed toward disaster. But it's in a very precarious situation right now."

Part of what makes Earth's situation so precarious is the planet's growing shortage of clean fresh-water resources. Although there is as much water on Earth today as there ever was, a growing human population has led to the increased use—and abuse—of this vital resource. People have over-consumed, diverted, and polluted the world's waters for generations, and today it is becoming increasingly difficult to find usable sources of fresh water, which many people fear will lead to a worldwide water crisis. But why are water resources becoming scarce? And what does that mean for our daily lives? Is there anything we can do to stop the water crisis before it's too late?

Without water, there would be no life on Earth. Plants, animals, and people all depend on water to sustain them. In fact, 60 to 70 percent of the human body is made up of water, and without water, a person would die within a few days. Water is necessary not only for drinking but also for cooking, cleaning, maintaining personal hygiene, and growing food.

CHAPTER ONE

A Life-Sustaining Cycle

Scientists estimate that there are about 332.5 million cubic miles (1.4 billion cu km) of water on Earth, covering nearly three-quarters of the planet's surface. If all the water on Earth were spread evenly over its surface, there would be enough to cover the entire planet to a depth of 1.7 miles (2.7 km). Most of this water is not readily available for human use, however, as 97 percent of it is salt water. Of the 3 percent that remains, about two-thirds is frozen in glaciers, ice caps, and **permafrost**. Another 30 percent of fresh water is stored in underground **reservoirs** called aquifers. An aquifer is an area of porous materials, such as sand or gravel, that are saturated with water. About 0.9 percent of the remaining fresh water can be found in the atmosphere, and only 0.3 percent is present as surface water, such as lakes or rivers.

No matter where it is found, all of Earth's water is involved in the hydrologic cycle, or water cycle. The water cycle constantly recycles our planet's water supply, pulling water from Earth's surface into the atmosphere and then returning it to the surface in the form of precipitation. This means that new water is never created and old water is never destroyed; the water simply changes states (from solid to liquid to gas) and location (from ocean to atmosphere to river). Because of this, water is considered a renewable resource.

The island of Kauai's Mt. Waialeale may be one of the wettest spots on Earth, but places a few miles away receive only 10 inches (25 cm) a year.

Once Europeans began exploring the Amazon River in the 1500s, the native peoples who had lived along its banks retreated farther inland.

Additionally, lakes, rivers, and aquifers are not found in equal abundance everywhere. Half of the world's freshwater supply is concentrated in just six countries—Brazil, Russia, Canada, Indonesia, China, and Colombia. Even countries that don't top the list in terms of water supply may have plenty of water available per capita (per person), depending on the size of their population. Greenland's 60,000 people, for example, could each use nearly 8 million gallons (30.3 million l) of water a day. In contrast, India is home to nearly 20 percent of the world's population but holds only 4 percent of the planet's fresh water. Other especially dry regions include the Middle East, North Africa, and Australia. Sometimes, regions may have a lot of fresh water, but it may not be easily accessible to many people. For example, the Amazon and Orinoco rivers in South America and the Congo River in Africa carry about a quarter of the world's available fresh water but pass through dense rainforests where few people live. Not many people live near enough to take advantage of the lengthy Lena and Yenisei rivers in the Siberian Arctic, either.

Viewing the Aral Sea from space, it is easy to see how much the body of water has shrunk, as its former borders are still visible.

Water World

Located between Kazakhstan and Uzbekistan, the Aral Sea was once the world's fourth-largest lake, but beginning in the 1960s, diversions of the rivers that feed into it caused the sea to gradually shrink. By 2004, it had lost two-thirds of its surface area, and the shoreline had receded as far as 155 miles (250 km) in some places. Abandoned ships were left to rust on the former lakebed, which had become a toxic desert. Although the outlook for the sea once appeared grim, in 2001, the Kazakh government and the World Bank began working to restore water flows to the sea. By 2009, sea levels had begun to rise.

CHAPTER TWO

Using and Abusing Water

Each one of the world's 6.8 billion people needs water every day. Although the average person needs at least 13 gallons (50 l) of water a day, people in some areas use much more than the minimum requirement. In fact, overconsumption of water resources is one of the leading causes of water scarcity and **degradation**, along with dams and diversions, pollution, and global warming.

Every day, the average person in the United States and Canada uses 100 to 151 gallons (379–572 l) of water. Only about one-third of a gallon (1.3 l) is used for drinking. The rest is used for flushing toilets, running appliances, bathing, and watering lawns and gardens. Although households can use a lot of water, worldwide they account for only about one-tenth of total water consumption. Another one-fifth of the world's water supply is used for industry, although in highly industrialized nations, industrial water use can account for more than half of total water consumption.

By far, the biggest global water guzzler is agriculture, which accounts for nearly three-quarters of all human freshwater usage. In some countries that have naturally drier climates, such as Egypt, Mexico, and Australia, agriculture can consume as much as 90 percent of the water extracted from rivers, lakes, and aquifers. In many parts of the world, farmers water their crops through flood **irrigation**, in which water is channeled to fields through canals, where rows of narrow, shallow trenches carry the water to plants. Much of the water used in flood irrigation is wasted, however, as it evaporates or seeps into the ground before reaching the crops. In addition, some crops require massive amounts of water, and many of these crops are grown in dry, water-scarce regions,

When it comes to irrigating fields, there are many options available to today's farmers, with some more efficient than others.

Water World

If North Americans use an average of 100 to 151 gallons (379–572 l) of water a day, with only one-third of a gallon (1.3 l) used for drinking, where does the rest go? A washing machine uses 40 gallons (151 l) of water per load, and a five-minute shower uses 10 gallons (38 l). Leaving the water running while brushing your teeth uses about 4 gallons (15 l), and flushing the toilet just once uses 1 to 3 gallons (3.8–11.4 l). Installing a low-flow toilet, turning off the tap while brushing your teeth, and taking shorter showers can all help to save water in the home.

A dam helps generate water power by directing falling water through pipes or tunnels called penstocks to hit turbines located below.

water sources across the world. Some of the chemicals come from industries, but others, including cleaners, antibacterial soaps, and medicines, flow from household drains. Other pollutants come from agriculture, as fertilizers and other nutrients run off of fields and into nearby waterways, eventually making their way to the ocean. There they can cause **eutrophication**, a process in which massive algae blooms sparked by an over-abundance of nutrients block sunlight from reaching aquatic plants, causing them to die. When the nutrients are used up, the algae also die, and as decomposers such as bacteria feed on the algae and dead plants, they deplete the water of oxygen, creating dead zones where no animal life can survive. One of the world's largest dead zones forms every spring and summer where the Mississippi River flows into the Gulf of Mexico, leaving 8,000 square miles (20,700 sq km) of water lifeless.

Global warming caused by the production of greenhouse gases appears to be a growing threat to Earth's water supply. Although some scientists disagree about the extent of global warming, many believe that Earth's surface temperature could increase by 2 to 11.5 °F (1 to 6.4 °C) over the next century. As a result, many of the world's glaciers could melt, causing the rivers they supply to at first overflow and then slow to a trickle. Warming temperatures and melting glaciers may also cause sea levels to rise and submerge coastal wetlands and cities.

Water World

In Africa, where women walk an average of four miles (6.4 km) to find usable water, an innovative new project is harnessing children's energy to supply water directly to local communities. The project involves the use of a water pump attached to a merry-go-round, called a PlayPump. PlayPumps are often installed near schools, and as schoolchildren spin the merry-go-round, the pump goes up and down, pulling water out of the ground and into a storage tank. So far, more than 1,000 PlayPumps have been installed in South Africa, Mozambique, Swaziland, Zambia, and other African countries, providing entertainment for children and water for their families.

In the summer months, during Sudan's long dry season, women can spend up to six hours a day finding enough water to carry home.

Human-induced changes to Earth's water supply can have dire consequences for people around the world. Today, more than a billion people—mostly in sub-Saharan Africa and Southeast Asia—do not have access to even a gallon (3.8 l) per day of clean, safe drinking water. In some places, scarce or depleted resources cause water shortages. Much of Africa, for example, is naturally dry. In other areas, people have access to water, but it is too polluted to be safe. In Pakistan, three-quarters of the population has no access to safe drinking water because so many of the country's water sources are polluted. Part of the reason that so much of the world's water is unsafe to drink is that 2.6 billion people around the world have no access to sanitation facilities. In the city of Jakarta, Indonesia, for example, 97 percent of homes are not connected to a sewer system, so waste flows directly into rivers, lakes, and groundwater sources.

CHAPTER THREE

A Dire Situation

Globally, contaminated water is the leading cause of sickness and death. Every year, three million people, most of them children under the age of five, die of water-related diseases. Drinking contaminated water can cause a host of illnesses, including cholera, typhoid, dysentery, and diarrhea. Other water-related diseases can be contracted when there is not enough water for basic hygiene or when a person comes into contact with a contaminated water supply. Such ailments may include scabies, trachoma, and typhus.

Depleted and polluted water sources can also affect the world's food supply. In the U.S., crop production in the High Plains region has decreased by half since the 1970s as the water table of the extensive Ogallala Aquifer—on which farmers rely

Open sewers are a common sight in many developing countries, with some on the outskirts of towns and others flowing in the streets.

When the Aswan High Dam was completed in 1970, it created the massive reservoir of Lake Nasser (right) on the Nile River (left).

for irrigation—has correspondingly dropped. Although irrigation is intended to water the land and make it more productive, too much water can have the opposite effect. If irrigated fields are not drained properly, the soil can become waterlogged, which causes underground salt deposits to be brought to the surface, forming an infertile crust on the land. Each year, more than 2.5 million acres (1 million ha) of farmland become unproductive because of **soil salination**. Other fields lose their fertility when dams prevent rivers from flooding and depositing nutrient-rich **silt** on farmland. Egypt's Aswan High Dam, for example, blocks the annual floods that once deposited silt in the Nile Delta. Because the silt is absent, farmers in the delta must now use high levels of chemical fertilizers to make up for the fact that the soil quality has declined.

Although Bogotá is serviced by a water sanitation company, poorer neighborhoods may not enjoy the same access to those services.

Water World

Around the world, wetlands have been filled in to make room for fields and cities, but today, many scientists are calling for the restoration of wetlands as the key to solving the world's water problems. Restored wetlands can help filter pollutants, retain surface water, recharge aquifers, and lessen the effects of floods. In Colombia, a high-elevation wetland known as the páramo supplies 70 percent of the city of Bogotá's drinking water. The wetland absorbs moisture and releases it at a steady rate year-round. It also filters the water, which usually has to be treated only with chlorine before being delivered to the city's nearly eight million inhabitants.

A dried up riverbed affords space for farming near Kanpur, India, but the toxic chemicals found in the soil can make products unhealthy.

Another danger to the world's food supply results from the use of polluted irrigation waters. The International Water Management Institute estimates that up to one-tenth of all the world's irrigated crops are watered with sewage. Other irrigation water is tainted with the industrial chemicals that filter into rivers and aquifers. Agricultural and dairy products produced near Kanpur, India, are contaminated with high levels of the heavy metals chromium and arsenic from nearby tanneries (factories where animal hides are made into leather), and vegetables grown near China's Yellow River show traces of the heavy metals lead, chromium, and cadmium. Such heavy metals are toxic to humans and can damage the nervous system, lungs, kidneys, and liver, and even cause cancer in some cases.

As water becomes scarce, there is also a growing threat of conflicts breaking out over who should have access to remaining water resources. In 2008, for example, the state of Montana sued the state of Wyoming for taking too much water from the **tributaries** of the Colorado River. In Klaten, Indonesia, the fight over water was not in the courtrooms; during the 2004 dry season, farmers armed themselves with axes, saws, and hammers before venturing out to water their crops, ready to engage in hand-to-hand combat instead, if need be.

Water World

The modern world's first full-scale water war was fought in 1967, when Israel defeated Syria, Egypt, and Jordan in the Six-Day War. Although this war was fought largely over land, water was also an issue. After Israel constructed a pipeline to carry the waters of the Jordan River across its countryside, Syria responded by beginning to dig canals on the Jordan's tributaries, attempting to access the water by a different means. The Israelis then bombed the canals. Ariel Sharon, a commander of Israeli troops during the war, later said, "While the border disputes were of great significance, the matter of water diversion was a stark issue of life and death."

With 261 large rivers flowing through more than one country worldwide, there is also much potential for international conflicts over water to occur, especially in the dry and politically unstable region of the Middle East. Between 1948 and 2002, there were at least 30 violent, isolated conflicts over water between Israel and its neighbors alone. Other potential flashpoints on an international scale include the Brahmaputra River in China and India, the Okavango water basin in Angola, Botswana, and Namibia, and the Indus River in India and Pakistan. Leaders in Egypt, a country that relies on the Nile River for 97 percent of its water, have threatened to go to war if the river is diverted by any of the nine East African countries that lie upstream.

While countries may sometimes threaten to fight over having too little water, the problems many human populations face come in the form of having too much water. Today, many of the world's worst floods are either caused or intensified by the presence of dams on rivers. In some cases, dams have failed, releasing floodwaters on communities downstream. In 2005, a 1,000-foot-wide (305 m) dam on Pakistan's Shadikor River gave way, drowning more than 100 people. Dams don't even have to fail to be a danger to people. Often, dam reservoir levels are kept high in order to provide more hydroelectricity or to supply irrigation systems. During periods of heavy rainfall, dam operators have to open spillways in order to prevent the dams from overflowing, and this action releases massive amounts of water downstream with no warning. The destruction of wetlands and floodplains for human development can also intensify the effects of floods. A healthy wetland can absorb much of the water spilled by rivers during floods, but when wetlands are drained and turned into housing or shopping developments, floodwaters have nowhere to go but through the developed area.

In 2008, disastrous floods affected many midwestern towns in the U.S., submerging or damaging homes, businesses, and schools.

Fishing is a communal activity and way of life
for many people who live along the world's
coastlines, such as this group in India.

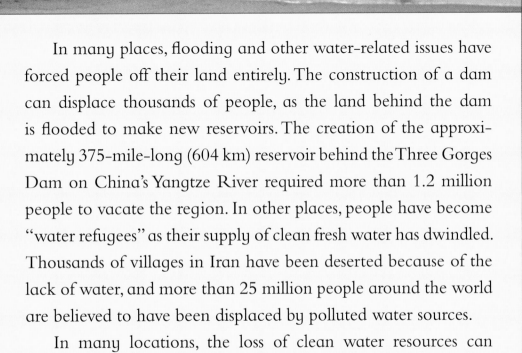

In many places, flooding and other water-related issues have forced people off their land entirely. The construction of a dam can displace thousands of people, as the land behind the dam is flooded to make new reservoirs. The creation of the approximately 375-mile-long (604 km) reservoir behind the Three Gorges Dam on China's Yangtze River required more than 1.2 million people to vacate the region. In other places, people have become "water refugees" as their supply of clean fresh water has dwindled. Thousands of villages in Iran have been deserted because of the lack of water, and more than 25 million people around the world are believed to have been displaced by polluted water sources.

In many locations, the loss of clean water resources can also mean a loss of food and income. Fishing of the world's coastal waters contributes an estimated $34 billion to the global economy annually, but eutrophication has caused a decline in **fisheries** in many coastal regions. Inland fisheries, too, are important, especially in the **developing world**, where they provide both income and a main source of protein for much of the population; as inland waters become polluted, the fish that live within them often die or become dangerous to consume.

According to the United Nations' (UN's) 2007 Global Environment Outlook report, if Earth's population continues to grow at present rates, two-thirds of the planet's people could face water stress by 2025, with demand for water outstripping the available supply. In recognition of the problem, the UN declared in 2003 that the years 2005 to 2015 would be the "Water for Life" decade. During that time period, the UN's goals include reducing the number of people who lack access to safe drinking water and basic sanitation by half, while also bringing an end to the unsustainable use of water resources.

CHAPTER FOUR

Renewing the Resource

One of the most basic ways to increase the available supply of fresh water is to encourage water conservation. Because the greatest quantity of water used in most parts of the world is for agriculture, many conservation efforts have begun to focus on growing "more crop per drop" by improving irrigation techniques. Drip irrigation, which delivers water through narrow pipes (either above or below ground) to areas near the roots of plants, can both reduce water usage and increase crop yields. In addition, scientists are working to develop new crop varieties that can be grown using less water.

Even with such agricultural advances, however, some scientists claim that it is foolhardy and wasteful to grow water-intensive crops such as cotton and rice in dry locations. The scientists say that these areas should instead import "virtual water," which is defined as the water used to grow and manufacture products. When dry countries purchase crops grown in other, wetter parts of the world, they are, in essence, also importing the water that was used to grow them instead of wasting their own limited

Grapes that grow on trellises can be watered conservatively using drip irrigation, with the irrigation tube woven along the vine row.

Sewage that enters a typical wastewater treatment plant goes through numerous steps to ensure that it exits in a clean, filtered state.

water supply. For example, growing a pound (0.45 kg) of wheat requires 130 gallons (492 l) of water, so for every pound (0.45 kg) of wheat they import, water-scarce countries save 130 gallons (492 l) of water. Already, Egypt, Iran, and Algeria import large amounts of virtual water in the form of food. Unfortunately, many countries do not have enough money to purchase large quantities of food from outside their borders, so the exchange of virtual water may not be feasible everywhere.

Another way to conserve water is to reuse or recycle it. The process of wastewater reclamation usually involves treating wastewater for use in flushing toilets, watering lawns, manufacturing goods, and irrigating crops. In some places, sewage can even be treated for eventual use as drinking water. In Orange County, California, for example, wastewater that has been purified to meet drinking water standards is injected into the ground, where it seeps into aquifers that supply the region's drinking water.

In some areas of the world, solving the problem of water shortages has been as simple as making better use of the rain that falls on the land. In Kenya, rainwater from rooftops is stored in large tanks for household use. In other places, such as India, where the majority of the rain for the year falls during the short monsoon season, villagers have dug huge ponds in which to store rainwater.

Cloud seeding can be accomplished more directly—and violently—with special guns loaded with silver-iodide-filled rockets.

Harvesting rainwater is one method of capturing atmospheric moisture. Another is to harvest fog. The Pacific coast of South America is dotted with huge mesh nets made of plastic, on which the moisture from fog condenses into water droplets that flow into a collection trough. The water is used to irrigate tree plantations and even supply villages with drinking water (after being filtered). Cloud seeding is a more technologically advanced solution to increasing the productivity of atmospheric moisture. Many cloud seeding projects involve spraying particles of silver iodide into clouds from airplanes or ground-based generators. The silver iodide particles are similar to ice crystals and cause the water droplets in clouds to condense and freeze around them.

Rice is an extremely water-intensive crop that nevertheless provides the backbone for the non-Western diet, which is rich in fiber.

Water World

In addition to the actual water you use each day for drinking, washing, cooking, and cleaning, you also consume a certain amount of "virtual water" in the foods you eat. The average person in the **Western** world whose diet is based on meat consumes about 1,320 gallons (5,000 l) of water a day in food products. Growing enough coffee to fill one cup requires 37 gallons (140 l) of water. A serving of rice uses 25 gallons (95 l) and a glass of milk 265 gallons (1,000 l), and growing enough grass to feed cattle and produce a hamburger requires 800 gallons (3,028 l) of water.

Eventually, they turn into snowflakes and fall to the ground as either rain or snow, depending on surface temperatures.

Another high-tech solution to water shortages can be found in desalination, a process through which salt is removed from seawater or **brackish** water to create fresh water. Although there are now approximately 22,000 desalination plants in 120 countries, most are small, and the fresh water they produce amounts to only one-tenth of one percent of total global water use. Because desalination is expensive, most plants are concentrated in wealthy nations, such as Saudi Arabia, which obtains nearly three-quarters of its drinking water from desalination plants. In addition to their expense, desalination plants create a hazardous mix of **brine** and chemicals that is often discharged into the sea.

Other countries have come up with their own high-tech solutions to the water crisis. In 2002, China began a massive project to divert the water of the Yangtze River nearly 800 miles (1,290 km) north to the dry North China Plain and its depleted Yellow River, and a similar project has been planned in India. Both projects are controversial, however, as environmentalists worry about the impact such drastic changes would have on the river basins and surrounding communities.

Even as some countries look for ways to reroute rivers, other countries are rethinking the diversionary tactics of the past. Dams on many rivers, especially in the U.S., are being removed to restore the natural pace of the rivers' currents. Some scientists have also begun to advocate for the strategic use of multiple small dams instead of a few large dams. They contend that a series of small dams placed on a river will cause fewer negative environmental effects and can benefit more people spread over a wider geographical area.

China's water diversion project will consist of three canals that cross the country's eastern, central, and western regions.

As they look for ways to restore a more natural environment, many nations have also passed laws to clean up water resources and make them usable again. The U.S. passed the Clean Water Act in 1972, and since then, many of the country's lakes, rivers, and other bodies of water have become noticeably cleaner. Under the regulations of the Clean Water Act, polluters can receive heavy fines. Some countries have implemented even harsher punishments. In 2006, the federal government of Malaysia declared that anyone found contaminating a water source in any way that could endanger lives would be put to death.

The many attempts to find solutions to the world's water crisis point to the truth of the proverb coined by Benjamin Franklin: "When the well is dry, we know the worth of water." In many parts of the world, the well is already dry, and more places may soon follow. But with careful conservation and cleanup, many experts believe that this is one environmental crisis that can be solved. As British environmental writer and consultant Fred Pearce points out, "The good news is that we never destroy water." No matter how much we reroute it, waste it, or pollute it, the total amount of water in the world never changes, and if we can learn to make better use of that water, there will be enough for everyone.

The Hudson River sloop *Clearwater* was built in 1969 and marked the founding of an environmental organization to protect the river.

Water World

In the 1960s, New York's Hudson River was a toxic soup of sewage, **nuclear** waste, and oil. The river changed colors each week, stained with dyes from a nearby General Motors plant. In 1966, people in the town of Crotonville formed the Hudson River Fishermen's Association, which later became Riverkeeper, to stop the river's polluters. Today, a Riverkeeper boat travels the Hudson to identify polluters and bring them to justice. As a result of Riverkeeper's efforts, hundreds of companies have been forced to clean up the Hudson, and additional "waterkeeper" programs have been founded on more than 180 waterways throughout the U.S. and around the world.

Water World

The bottled water industry today brings in $46 billion a year by promoting bottled water as a healthy, sustainable alternative to tap water. However, the truth is that a quarter of all bottled water is tap water, and in many countries, bottled water is held to lower purity standards than is tap water. In some cases, bottled water is contaminated, and one U.S. company's bottled water was actually taken from a well near a hazardous waste dump. In addition, millions of gallons of water are used to produce the plastic bottles that contain bottled water, and 90 percent of those bottles end up in landfills.

When using bottled water while camping, at a game, or on the road, people should recycle the bottles so the plastic can be reused.

Glossary

atmosphere—the layer of gases that surrounds Earth

brackish—salty, as in the mixture of fresh river water and seawater

brine—water with a very high concentration of salt

degradation—the process of breaking down or declining in quality

developing world—having to do with the poorest countries of the world, which are generally characterized by a lack of health care, nutrition, education, and industry; most developing countries are in Africa, Asia, and Latin America

eutrophication—the process by which the excessive increase of nutrients in a body of water (typically due to runoff from the land) leads to the growth and eventual decomposition of plants, reducing oxygen in the water and leading to the death of animal life

evaporate—to change from a liquid into a gas, or vapor, usually from the application of heat

fisheries—areas of a body of water where fish are caught, often for commercial purposes

hydroelectricity—electricity created by using flowing or falling water to drive a turbine, which is connected to a generator

irrigation—the distribution of water to land or crops to help plant growth

molecules—the smallest units of a substance that retain the characteristics of that substance; molecules are made up of one or more atoms

nuclear—having to do with energy created when atoms are split or joined together

permafrost—a permanently frozen layer of soil below Earth's surface, usually found in the polar regions

reservoirs—places where water is stored, such as a man-made lake

sediment—tiny particles of matter carried by water or wind and deposited on the land or left to settle to the bottom of a body of water

silt—very fine particles of mud or clay carried by rivers and deposited as sediment

soil salination—a condition in which the excessive build-up of salts causes soil to decline in quality

spawning—the act of depositing eggs

transpiration—the process by which water vapor passes through the pores of plant leaves or stems and is released into the atmosphere

tributaries—streams or rivers that feed into larger rivers or lakes

water tables—levels below which groundwater can be found

Western—having to do with the part of the world that includes Europe and the Americas

wet monsoon—a large-scale wind system in Southeast Asia and India that blows from May through September and brings heavy rains

Bibliography

Alters, Sandra M. *Water: No Longer Taken for Granted*. Detroit: Thomson Gale, 2008.

Barlow, Maude. *Blue Covenant: The Global Water Crisis and the Coming Battle for the Right to Water*. New York: The New Press, 2007.

De Villiers, Marq. *Water: The Fate of Our Most Precious Resource*. Boston: Houghton Mifflin, 2000.

Millennium Ecosystem Assessment. *Ecosystems and Human Well-Being: Wetlands and Water Synthesis*. Washington, D.C.: World Resources Institute, 2005.

Pearce, Fred. *When the Rivers Run Dry: Water—The Defining Crisis of the Twenty-First Century*. Boston: Beacon Press, 2006.

Postel, Sandra. "From the Headwaters to the Sea." *Environment* 47, no. 10 (December 2005): 8–21.

Stein, Richard Joseph, ed. *Water Supply*. New York: H. W. Wilson Company, 2008.

Ward, Diane Raines. *Water Wars: Drought, Flood, Folly, and the Politics of Thirst*. New York: Riverhead Books, 2002.

For Further Information

Books

Bowden, Rob. *Water Supply: Our Impact on the Planet*.
Austin, Tex.: Raintree Steck-Vaughn, 2003.

Fridell, Ron. *Protecting Earth's Water Supply*.
Minneapolis: Lerner Publications, 2009.

Silverman, Buffy. *Saving Water: The Water Cycle*.
Chicago: Heinemann Library, 2008.

Spilsbury, Louise, and Richard Spilsbury. *Water*.
Chicago: Heinemann Library, 2007.

Web Sites

Grinning Planet: Water Pollution Facts
http://www.grinningplanet.com/2005/07-26/water-pollution-facts-article.htm

H2ouse: Water Saver Home
http://www.h2ouse.org

United Nations CyberSchoolBus Water Quiz
http://cyberschoolbus.un.org/waterquiz/waterquiz4/index.asp

Water Pollution Guide
http://www.water-pollution.org.uk

Index

A

Africa 12, 22, 24, 30, 37
   PlayPumps 22
animals 6, 33, 39
atmosphere 4, 6, 10, 18
Australia 12, 14

B

Canada 12, 14, 15
   and water usage 14, 15
China 12, 18, 29, 30, 33, 40
   Three Gorges Dam 33
conservation measures 9, 15, 34, 37,
    38, 40, 42, 43
   cloud seeding 38
   desalination 40
   harvesting fog 38
   increasing water prices 9
   laws 42
   rainwater storage 37, 38
   Riverkeeper organization 43
   wastewater reclamation 37

E

Egypt 14, 26, 30
energy 17, 18, 30
Engelman, Robert 4
eutrophication 21, 33

F

flooding 26, 27, 30, 33

G

greenhouse gases 4, 18, 21
   carbon dioxide 4
   methane 18

H

habitats 4, 12, 18, 27, 30
health endangerment 24
   water-related diseases 24

I

India 10, 12, 17, 18, 29, 30, 37, 40
   wet monsoon season 10, 37
Indonesia 12, 24, 29
International Water Management
   Institute 29

M

Mexico 14, 18
   and subsidence issues 18
Middle East 12, 30, 33, 37, 40

P

Pearce, Fred 42
plant life 4, 6, 8, 14, 17, 21, 29, 34, 37, 39
   transpiration 8
   water-intensive crops 17, 34, 37
populations 5, 12, 14, 17, 24, 27, 30,
    33, 34
   displaced 33
   and water per person 12, 14, 24

R

rainfall by location 10

S

South America 10, 12, 18, 27, 38

U

United Nations 2007 Global
   Environment Outlook 34
United States 10, 14, 15, 17, 29, 37, 40,
    42, 43, 44
   Clean Water Act 42
   and water usage 14, 15

V

virtual water 34, 37, 39

W

water cycle 6, 8, 10, 14, 17, 30, 37, 40
   evaporation 8, 10, 14, 17
   evapotranspiration 8, 10
   precipitation 6, 8, 10, 30, 37, 40

water shortages 4, 5, 13, 14, 17, 18, 21,
    24, 26, 29, 30, 33, 37, 40, 42, 43
   affecting food supply 24, 29
   causes 4, 5, 13, 14
    dams 14, 17, 18, 26, 30, 33, 40
    diversion 4, 5, 13, 14, 17, 18, 30,
     40, 42
    global warming 14, 18, 21
    overconsumption 5, 14, 42
    pollution 5, 14, 18, 21, 24, 29, 42,
     43
     sources 18, 21, 29, 43
   conflicts 29, 30
water sources 4, 6, 8, 10, 12, 13, 14, 17,
    18, 21, 24, 26, 27, 29, 30, 33, 34, 37,
    40, 42, 43
   aquifers 6, 8, 10, 12, 14, 18, 24, 27,
    29, 37
   glaciers 6, 21
   groundwater 18, 24
   lakes 6, 8, 10, 12, 13, 14, 18, 24, 42
    Aral Sea 13
    Lake Superior 10
   oceans 6, 8, 10
   reservoirs 17, 18, 30, 33
   rivers 4, 6, 8, 10, 12, 13, 14, 17, 18,
    21, 24, 26, 29, 30, 40, 42, 43
   salt water 6, 18, 40
   vapor 8, 10
water supply 6, 10, 12, 14, 15, 17, 18, 21,
    22, 24, 26, 29, 30, 33, 34, 37, 38,
    39, 44
   accessibility 12, 24
   amount globally 6
   availability 12, 18, 21, 34
   blue versus green water 10
   used by agriculture 14, 17, 18, 26,
    29, 30, 34, 37, 38
    irrigation 14, 18, 26, 29, 30, 34,
     37, 38
   used by households 14, 15, 17, 22,
    34, 37, 38, 39
   used by industry 14, 17, 33, 37, 44